Help Meadow

Save the Day!

Andrew Pollack Julie Pollack Lisa Britton

Illustrations by Lisa Britton

Help Meadow Save the Day!

Andrew Pollack, Julie Pollack & Lisa Britton
Illustrations by Lisa Britton

Printed in the USA
Published in the USA

This book is dedicated to Meadow Jade Pollack.
As the youngest in her family, she was
affectionately known as Princess.
Her personality, beauty and style befitted her title.
She lived by her motto: “Be kind to all kinds”.

Meadow was 18 years old and soon to begin her
college career when she became one of the
17 victims of the Marjory Stoneman Douglas High School massacre
on February 14, 2018.
At the end, she heroically shielded a younger student.
She is loved and remembered by her family and friends every day.
Her strength and grace will always be an inspiration.

Help Meadow
Save the Day!
Andrew Pollack Julie Pollack Lisa Britton
Illustrations by Lisa Britton
K9 MEADOW

I am a working dog
with a very special job...

K9 MEADOW

I work hard
to keep children
safe!

Before I became a working dog,

I was
rescued!

I trained with

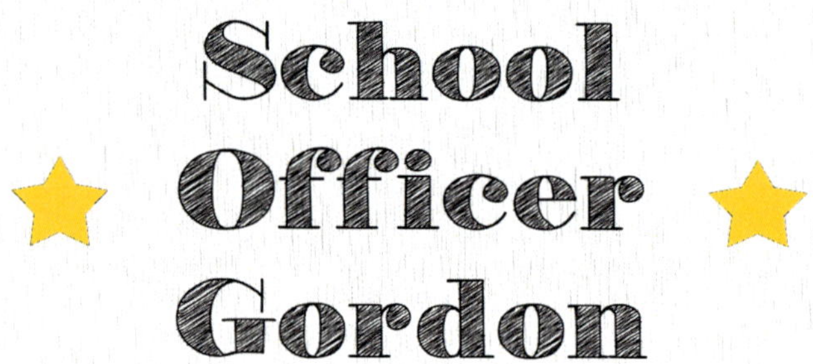

to become healthy and strong.

Safety
First

Now I
go to
school...

Just like you!

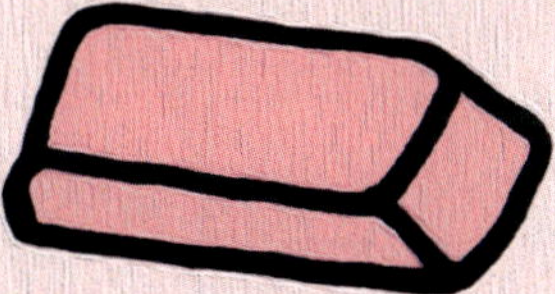

Security Camera: 1 rec
10/24 9:48 AM
K9 MEADOW
Sniff!
Sniff!
SEE SOMETHING SAY SOMETHING!

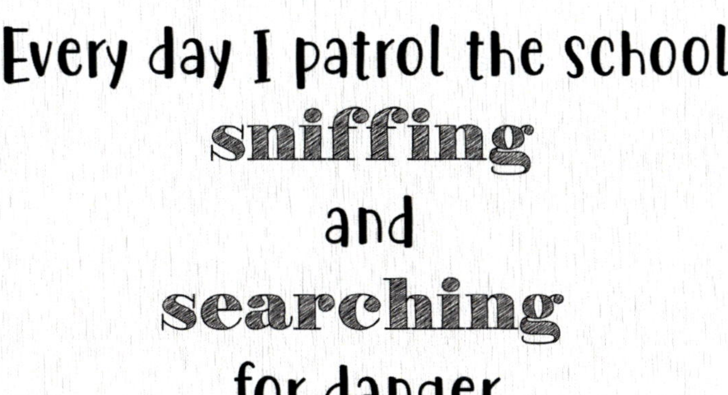

Every day I patrol the school,
sniffing
and
searching
for danger.

I have been trained
to detect anything suspicious.

(My nose is stronger than
School Officer Gordon's!)

Know that if you have a worry
or just need a friend

you can **always** come to us!

I work very hard to keep you safe at school, and you can be a hero too!

You can help me **SAVE THE DAY!**

We can all work together

to make our
school a safe
place to
work
and
play.

The first step is easy:
like me,
you must be **alert!**

If you **see something**
that looks dangerous...

say something

so no one gets hurt!

If you hear a friend say something odd

which might seem like a **threat,**

They'll regret this!

it's not tattling to tell a teacher...

Getting them
help
is the best bet!

ABC

The next step is a little bit harder:
you might have to stand up to friends.
When kids are bullying others
it's important to make sure that it ends!

Bullying can be contagious;
it's easy to just join in.
Classmates may want to copy like parrots,
but that's not the way we win.

SAFETY
FIRST

Make sure you tell a parent,
or any adult at school!

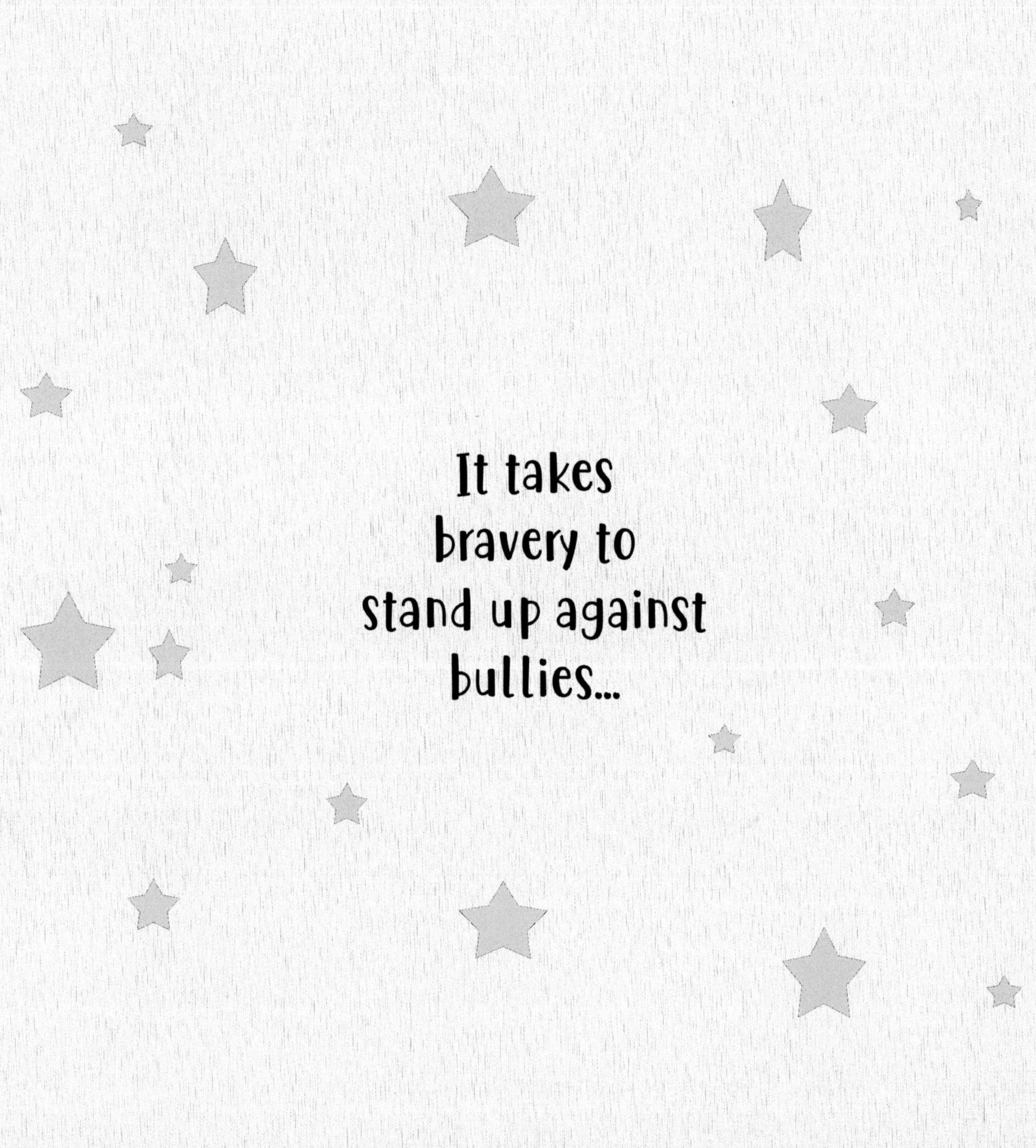

It takes
bravery to
stand up against
bullies...

picking on others isn't cool!

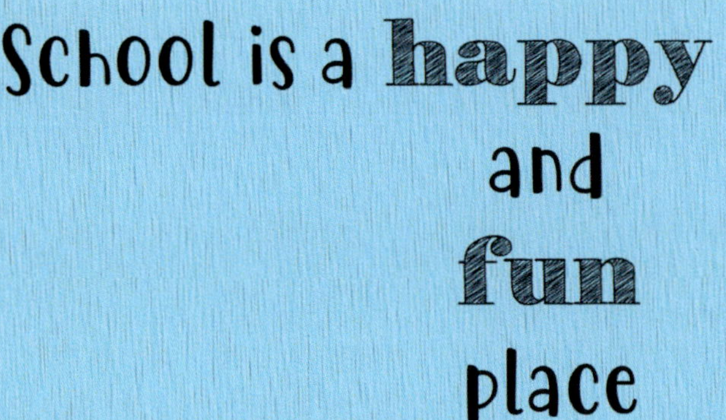

School is a **happy**
and
fun
place

where children learn and play.

If you help me **patrol** and stay **alert**,
we'll keep it safe every day!

K9 MEADOW

In the aftermath of the Parkland shooting, Andrew and Julie Pollack found themselves searching for solutions to make schools safer. Parents and students are an important part of the process. Parents can pressure school officials to prioritize school safety and engage their children in conversation. Students are truly on the front lines of creating a positive and safe school environment. They need to be empowered and know that if they "See Something, Say Something."
#fixit

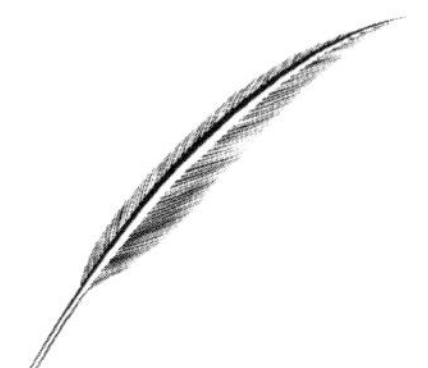

Lisa Britton is a children's book author from Los Angeles, CA. She is on a mission to empower ALL children. Her books address issues we deal with in society today. She believes that if we empower girls AND boys today, they will all have a better tomorrow.
#TheFutureIsEveryone

Made in the USA
Columbia, SC
02 January 2020